Praises

Through research, extensive coaching experience and speaking engagements, Nancy has perfected simple to use methods for individuals contemplating or going through career transitions. She provides examples of how her proven practices have helped clients decided what types of careers they'd 'really' like and ways of obtaining them. This book is a must read for anyone going through a career change!
JC Heinen, SVP
Leadership Development Practice

When it comes to helping executives find their passion and pursue their dreams, no one is better than Nancy Sullivan. Whether moving up within an organization, moving out or changing careers entirely, Nancy has helped a countless number of successful leaders navigate career transitions and find professional success and fulfillment.
Jeffrey R. Tarr, CEO
DigitalGlobe

Nancy is a top notch coach who provided me with insight and helped me to see my options from an entirely different perspective. Being a CEO for 30 plus years does not necessarily qualify you to manage your own important career transitions, Nancy made a huge and positive difference in the course I chose.
Bill, CEO
Healthcare company

Nancy worked with several of my top leaders and was instrumental in assisting them to prepare for promotion and sometimes making lateral moves that were not only beneficial to the organization, but also propelled them to greater success in their own careers.
Mike, CEO
Energy company

If you have ever experienced Nancy as a speaker on career management you know what it's really like to find your passion and recognize how to take control of your destiny! Dynamic and extremely knowledgeable speaker—a transformative event every time she gets on stage.
P. McCullough, SVP
Technology company

Nancy's approach to career transition is a game changer. Her ability to go beyond the scope of change and manage the stress of change while maintaining the dignity of her client are skills few transition leaders possess. Nancy's presentation skills reveal her true depth of higher level thinking which capture the attention of everyone in the audience.
Bob Beeman, MBA, VP
Workforce Solutions
Apollo Education Group

TRANSITION POINTS

TRANSITION POINTS

Finding Your Career Intersection of Skill and Passion

NANCY SULLIVAN

 Little Gems Press

TransitionPoints: The Series
Published by Little Gems, Inc.

Copyright © 2015 by Nancy Sullivan. All rights reserved.

No part of this book may be reproduced in any written, electronic, recording, or photocopying form without written permission of the publisher or author. The exception would be in the case of brief quotations embodied in the critical articles and reviews and pages where permission is specifically granted by the publisher, Little Gems, or the author, Nancy Sullivan.

Although every precaution has been taken to verify the accuracy of the information contained herein, the author and publisher assume no responsibility for any errors or omissions. No liability is assumed for damages that may result from the use of information contained within.

TransitionPoints may be purchased singularly or in bulk in hardcopy or electronic form from Amazon.com or hardcopy at any bookstore.

Cover Design: Nick Zelinger, NZ Graphics
Interior Design: Ronnie Moore, WESType Publishing Services
Editor: John Maling, EditingByJohn.com
Book Consultant: Judith Briles, TheBookShepherd.com

ISBN 978-0-9960861-1-0 (paper)
ISBN 978-0-9960861-2-7 (digital)

LCCN: Data on File

1. Business.   2. Careers.   3. Change.

First Edition
Printed in the United States of America

Contents

Acknowledgments	ix
1 What Is Your Career?	3
2 Where Are You in Your Career?	17
3 What Do You Want?	33
4 Finding Your Career Intersection of Skill and Passion	45
5 Making Choices in Your Career	65
6 Managing Your Career	85
7 Transition Points	107
Final Word	113
About the Author	115
Working with Nancy Sullivan	117

Acknowledgments

Nothing is created by a single person or entity, and that includes getting books written. If not for all of the support, input, patience and mentoring I received, this book would still be languishing in my head and on my desk!

My entire family has been so supportive, always encouraging me and also pushing me forward when I got stuck—especially my husband Ric. His patience and understanding when I would spend weekends at my desk instead of in the woods camping with him was appreciated beyond what I could ever say.

The material in *TransitionPoints* is largely composed of experiences I have had over the past several years with clients, colleagues and the many people going through change and transition in their careers. I owe all of you for helping me to move forward, learn and experience the challenges and triumphs as you courageously made decisions, set priorities and continued to look for your career intersection of excellence and passion.

A final thank you to my Book Shepherd, Judith Briles. Without her relentless support and drive to completion, this book would never have seen the light of day.

Many thanks to all!

*If you are not who, what or where you want to be,
you are at a Transition Point…
Make the Transition NOW.*

—Nancy Sullivan

When you are inspired by some great purpose, some extraordinary project, all your thoughts break their bonds: Your mind transcends limitations, your consciousness expands in every direction, and you find yourself in a new, great, and wonderful world. Dormant forces, faculties and talents become alive, and you discover yourself to be a greater person by far than you ever dreamed yourself to be.

—Patanjali – the author of *Yoga Sutra*

What Is Your Career?

CHAPTER 1

Each man has his own vocation; his talent is his call. There is one direction in which all space is open to him.
—Ralph Waldo Emerson

Chuck's Story

At Lee Hecht Harrison, a series of workshops are provided for individuals going through career transition. Within them, participants are able to hear speakers with expertise in various fields, network and gain peer referrals.

I was asked to speak to a group of senior level leaders who had all left their employers, either by choice or at the direction of the organization. This can be a very stressful time for individuals, some have not looked for a job in 20 plus years, and many never had to apply for a job because they had always been sought out by someone to join an organization.

As I looked out on the audience, I saw a mixed group of very experienced senior leaders—some of whom had lost their anchor income. In too many cases, they had lost a sense of who they really were. They could no longer define themselves by their current position; they didn't have one. Others were young, very successful leaders who followed a path in an organization with high hopes of greater income, flexibility and sometimes a belief in the purpose of their employer's vision. These individuals were disillusioned about the workplace and uncertain about their next steps. How could they have been let go?

The discussion for the day was *Defining Your Career Options*. I spoke about some of the topics within this book—how important it was to understand what they wanted in their career, what was important to them and also to pay attention to what they really wanted from their career. There were many questions about how to discover what they really wanted to do, rather than concentrating on what they had been doing or what they had gone to school to do.

As the program ended, many milled around and shared leads and insights. Chuck approached me. He was in the Baby Boomer generation, well-dressed and very much the corporate image of a successful professional. His expression, however, was tense and pale.

"I enjoyed the discussion today, but I think I have a unique situation," he said. I asked him to elaborate and Chuck shared his story.

I come from a family of successful people. My dad was a senior government official who worked at the top levels of the Pentagon for more than forty years, hired right out of college. My mom was a stay-at-home mom during the years my brothers and I were young and then went back to college to get an MBA. One of my brothers is a well-respected dentist and the other is an attorney. We were told from the time we were small that college was not an option but an expectation. We were also lucky to have parents who supported us and really believed we were gifted with intelligence and could achieve great things in life.

I nodded, as I have heard many such strong backgrounds supporting leaders we identify as truly successful. "Sounds like a great family and that all of you have achieved great things!"

Yes, we are all successful if you define it in the traditional sense. I am a CPA and was a top Division Head at a multi-billion dollar company and had been there for about twenty-two years. I had expected to retire there. I have a big house in a terrific neighborhood and have five children, two are in college and three are in high school, now considering which college they will attend. We have a lot of responsibility to support them so they can be successful too.

I thought I had everything pretty well figured out and under control until we got a new CEO who reorganized the company and brought in his own senior leadership team. Overnight, I was replaced by one of his people he brought into the company.

Immediately, I engaged in services offered to help me transition to the next role and felt pretty good about my resume and followed the steps in the process to move ahead to my next corporate role. As I worked with my career coach, I shared that I didn't feel really motivated by any of the opportunities out there. It all seemed like *I've been there, done that* ... even though she has been really good at showing me other options I might have.

Honestly though, I am a CPA. From the time I was in grade school, my folks had told me how great I was at numbers. I excelled in math, calculus and accounting and I used to really enjoy making a spread sheet sing—it was like problem solving through numbers. I graduated college, earned my CPA credentials and achieved everything I thought I wanted.

"It sounds like maybe something changed for you?" I asked, seeing the look of angst on his face.

I don't know if it is this process or something that has been boiling up for a lot of months, maybe even years. For a long time I have dreaded going to work. I lived for the weekends when my family and I could go hiking, biking—pretty much anything to get me away from thinking about work. After listening to your talk today and contemplating the last few years, I have to ask myself, 'What am I doing here?' I have not enjoyed my job for a long time. I don't have any energy to put into it anymore. What happened?

It's an excellent question. Chuck had been directed into his profession through focus on what everyone told him he did well. He enjoyed the accolades, high salary and prestige of being a CPA for a long time, but realized at some point, he no longer enjoyed doing this work. He became bored and less engaged in his own job, and as he later admitted, had not been performing at the level he knew he could—and should. He then was not valued for his contributions (considered less than necessary by the new CEO) and was replaced.

Through discussions with his career coach and taking the time to focus on what really gave him energy, he was able to transfer his skills (which he thought only qualified him to be a "numbers guy") and found that his systematic way of thinking and problem solving was a highly sought after commodity in the energy industry.

In his quest for a new position, he found a new role at a senior level, leading a group of engineers working on solving safety issues for the organization. With a renewed sense of energy, he was able to leverage his great problem solving skills to accomplish something far more important than building spreadsheets (which he felt he had been doing). Through his new work, the organization avoided loss of human lives and provided greater protection for thousands of people.

I reconnected with Chuck a year after his transition. Energy-wise, he was different. He shared, "I have never felt so good about the work I do. Maybe this would not have been as important earlier in my career, but I really discovered that what motivated me then had changed— I just didn't recognize it until I got physically pushed out of my job. I wish I had recognized and responded to my lack of energy a lot sooner."

Chuck's story is not unusual. He reached a Transition Point, though he didn't realize it at the time, action was needed on his part. Chuck only required the right tools that would allow him to make the transition desired, in his own time.

As you read, you will discover tools to help you make your own transition, in your own time.

What Is Your Career?

Do you want a job that you can leave at 4 or 5 p.m. and never take work home with you? Do you want a career that will take you to your ultimate destination, whether that is a CEO, published research scientist, building a company from scratch, or even a principal of a school? Or, has your career changed over time or are you just not sure what you want, at least right now, today? Given that we spend countless thousands of hours working, it is surprising that so many of us never really step back to think seriously about consciously creating a meaningful and fulfilling career.

I have been working as a career coach and executive coach for more than 10 years, and before that I was Executive Director at a Fortune 500 telecommunications company where I ran multiple teams and was responsible for the P&L of many.

I knew most areas of the business—from operations to new product development and customer experience. After leaving my role at the telecom company, I ran my own business and worked with two start-up dot com companies as well. In summary, I have not only worked with executives in many industries and companies, but have held many diverse roles, from entry level supervisor to senior level executive to business owner.

I didn't start at the top; I worked my way up, working with a variety of executives along the way. Every employee starts somewhere—in a clerical or janitorial position; or at non-management; or at a mid-management position … the commonality is: they started. Some will love the next 20, 30 or even 60 years of working, and others will slog through it living for weekends and retirement.

As a coach, I've worked with people at various stages of their career. Some are in the earlier stages, bursting with enthusiasm; others, farther along, are exhausted and overwhelmed, wondering if they had gone down the right path in the first place. Over the decades, working with extraordinarily successful individuals I've learned this simple truth:

> It is difficult for most people to know exactly what they want out of a career … for some, it is difficult to even begin to think about it.

Why? Most of us just don't think about what we really want in the long term. Rather, we focus on things like: what money we want or need at the moment, a job that matches what we studied in college, or a job that is just easy or convenient.

Our career paths take many directions. Some start on what I call a "self-directed" path. From a young age, these people have a true sense of exactly what they want to be or do. It might be a firefighter, doctor, veterinarian or a mom. Regardless of the direction, they are lucky enough to know and follow the direction of their dreams. At the other end of the spectrum are those who are on an "other directed" path. Think about kids who get drilled into their heads from an early age that when they grow up they will be "X." Maybe it's a doctor, lawyer or even running the family business. This often happens when people see a great talent or capability in a child; perhaps the child is excellent at math, or does a great job building things. The constant accolades and support sometimes lead to believing that this is a "natural" career direction. Being a good kid, and not thinking there is any other option, the kid becomes the doctor, the lawyer or moves into the family business. Sometimes this works and the career path others had envisioned for that child is actually satisfying. However, at other times the results are not so great.

Bored. Not knowing why … or maybe not ever realizing boredom has become their way of life—the routine that they march to, day after day after day goes on. Then, something happens.

- ✦ A health crisis—you didn't understand that you were under a tremendous level of stress with your current position. During your recovery, you finally stepped away and started asking yourself questions: *Why am I doing this? What have I been doing for all this time? Why …?*
- ✦ A close friend or family member experiences a crisis or dies—you suddenly realized that the

shadow of that person who directed you into this career path was lifted and then the questions begin ... *Why do I do this? Why have I been doing this for 25 years ... Why ...?*
✦ Out of the blue, the pink slip arrives ... you're fired, laid off or "downsized." Truth be told, you really weren't engaged ... for the past 10 years, you coasted just under the radar. *Why me? Why was I called out, after all, I showed up, didn't I? Why ...?*

After working with hundreds of people in various careers, industries and at various stages, I have found that most of us follow what I call the "opportunistic" path. We are presented (or stumble upon) seemingly random opportunities throughout our lives and if it feels good or works for the moment, we take the opportunity. This too can work well if we make good choices but could be even better if we had a clearer sense of all the components that make this the "right" choice.

The purpose of *TransitionPoints: Finding Your Career Intersection of Skill and Passion* is to ***wake up!*** Stop working in a role or place you do not enjoy or belong. Your work is a big part of your life; don't let it cause you stress, tension and ultimately health issues. Throughout this book you will begin to answer the following questions:

✦ What is your career?
✦ Where is your career right now?
✦ What do you really want to be?

- What are you really good at?
- What do you really love doing?

Everyone has different needs and desires. Too often, however, few of us pay attention to or think intentionally about managing our career. The result is that we spend years in an unsatisfying career or mindless job-hopping. One job is replaced with another, without intentionally guiding our career, or understanding what happened at the last job and how that informs us as to what we want from the next job.

> **Job-hopping can be a good thing—when there is intentional, positive movement—when we *move to something* vs. *away from something*.**

As the millennial generation becomes more heavily represented in the job market, we are indeed seeing a shorter tenure at any given role. Gone are the days of working for a pension. (Who even offers one anymore?) We do understand that this generation looks at a job more as a project than a long term investment. But even for this generation, being clear about what you want from each job or role is important to ensure that you are investing your time in the best possible way to meet your present and future needs and goals. Career or job movement can result in a fulfilling career; however, I have worked with many who get stuck along the way. They end up in jobs or careers that drain their energy, do not bring them the results they really want, that are just plain boring, or maybe just don't "feel right" anymore.

Does that sound like you?

Another way of looking at work is to be mindful of that fact that you will work for roughly 8 to 10 hours a day, five days a week or more ... for 10, 20, 30, 40 years or more! Would you rather spend this time in *misery* or *compliance mode* or just *coasting*, or would you like to be *excited* every day, looking forward to the day's work and the difference you could be making through your work?

Transition Point

You spend many of your waking hours working. It is up to you how those hours are spent. By taking conscious and proactive control, it is possible to create the career of your dreams.

*If you don't know where you are going,
any road will get you there.*

—Lewis Carroll

Where Are You in Your Career?

CHAPTER 2

A journey of a thousand miles must begin with a single step.

—Lao Tzu

Raj's Story

Raj came from a family steeped in professional accomplishment. His father was a surgeon, his mother an attorney and his two sisters were successful business owners. I met Raj when he was referred to me by Pat, a good friend and CEO of a company in Denver.

Pat was a member of the YPO (Young Presidents' Organization) and knew many emerging leaders at various organizations. He had known Raj for several years and had great respect for the business Raj headed as a young President. During the four year course of their friendship, Raj had grown his business by more than 200 percent; it had just recently launched a global initiative that would undoubtedly accelerate its growth.

Raj was aggressive, driven and wise beyond his years. He had managed around difficult business situations and always drove the company to new levels of excellence. But over the past year, Raj changed. Pat noticed that he seemed drained and disengaged—even while his business achieved greater and greater success. Pat referred him to me to discuss his situation.

Raj started by sharing a bit about his background. "My business is enormously successful; the CEO has nothing but praise for my accomplishments and looks at me to be his successor in the next three to five years. My parents, who told me since I was small that I could accomplish anything, take great pride in my success and speak of me often to family and friends in India. I have a large home in a prestigious area of the city and my children go to the best private schools money can buy. My wife has never worked outside the home and takes great pride in raising our children to be responsible adults."

I marveled at his comfortable style and humble disposition in spite of his great accomplishments. "Sounds like you have it made Raj, but Pat has noticed a change in you over the past several months. What's going on?"

"I don't know. I used to get up every morning with great energy. I was proud of what I did, and it seemed like I could work for hours into the night and then get up with just a couple of hours of sleep. Lately though, I look forward to the weekends and some days can barely make it all the way through the day. I often dream about taking a vacation with my family—and not coming back."

Raj was clearly disengaged from his work, and after confirming he was in good health, we started to discuss what gave him the most energy, not only in his current role, but also in other areas of his life. We discussed his various career experiences and some of the more intangible behaviors he had mastered. As we talked about his past career and the roles he had played, a pattern emerged. Raj had always been motivated to succeed. Even in high school he was driven to be at the top with the highest academic honors, as a strong athlete and the president of Student Council. That focus was rewarding to Raj, and he would always strive for more. In talking about those accomplishments, Raj sighed as he came to face the reality that what had given him such energy and success in the past no longer fueled him.

Raj's conundrum was that he couldn't pinpoint what now would give him that same drive and sense of satisfaction. We worked through some processing about his current state of mind, and he also completed several assessments targeted at identifying his drivers and motivators and how he now defined success.

This transition point was very difficult for Raj to navigate; it called into question so much of how he had defined himself. It was important to include Raj's wife in the conversation, because as it became clear that a major shift was occurring, he recognized that this could also impact her and their children. After several months and deep reflection on his part, Raj determined that he was no longer motivated by moving up.

Investigation into alternative roles and organizational levels revealed that Raj felt hollow in his current role, while he was making great money (for himself and the company), and had achieved financial and personal recognition, the outcomes meant very little. He felt that he was not making a valuable contribution to his community, nor was he creating a legacy he would want to pass along to his young children. "Anyone can make a lot of money, what difference does that make at the end of the day? Children still starve in our own city, crime continues to grow and I just go on with my focus on making more money."

Raj had transitioned from a laser focus on upward mobility to needing to make a difference in another way. He started out thinking that he needed to leave the company, but after much discussion he determined that his own company could contribute in a great way to the community. Their technology was powerful and could be leveraged to support the school system, enabling students, particularly in poverty stricken areas, to have access to software and tools they could never afford. The technology could also go far in advancing the skills of many school age children. Raj also became aware that regulatory barriers existed making it more difficult to introduce the technology on a widespread basis.

The next step in Raj's journey would be to speak with his CEO about his changing focus. Key to his success was to offer an alternative plan wherein Raj would create a new role of Chief Community Strategy Officer and would focus on increasing political advocacy, and expanding the visibility of his organization in academic circles and as a leader in their technology space for 'making a difference'. Given his leadership and organizational skills, the business case was strong and while the CEO was taken aback with the news, he eventually supported the new role and began the search for an alternative successor. Raj shifted from a career position of Upwardly Mobile to Lateral Movement. There was an impact to initial compensation, but that sacrifice was nothing in comparison to the sense of fulfillment and renewed energy Raj received.

As with Raj's experience, there are always signs of an impending personal change. Things become less comfortable and satisfying and often a sense of anxiousness emerges. Raj was fortunate to have a network around him to support and enable him to make a major career shift, but in the end it was his openness to the possibility of a transition that resulted in his success.

In this chapter, a metamorphous occurs. You will walk through the process Raj undertook to move from an unsatisfying and unfulfilling career position to one that fueled his energy and leveraged his great skills and talent.

Where Are You in Your Career?

To start, it is necessary to look at where you are in your career. Are you miserable, coasting, excited about moving up or exploring other options, or are you just at a place where you are wondering if this is all there is, wondering what's next? Regardless of where you believe you are, or if you are not certain, the Career Position Model is a great place to start to get clarity.

The Career Position Model has five components. It's a quick and easy analysis, beginning with "X" marks the spot: "I am here." Don't make it complicated. Simply ask yourself: where am I? The Model consists of:

- ✦ Upward Mobility
- ✦ Deceleration Position
- ✦ Lateral Movement
- ✦ Outward Exit
- ✦ Enriching or Enhancing the Present

Upward Mobility

For those who are in Upward Mobility, it means wanting to move up within the organization (or to find an organization with opportunities to move up) to gain influence, more status or responsibility.

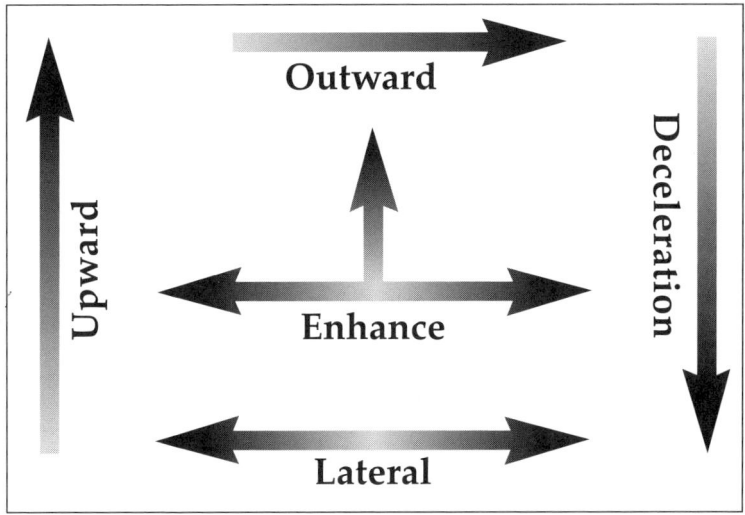

You may have been groomed to achieve, have more freedom, gain status, or simply to have more—a bigger car, more money, bigger job, bigger career, or work for a better company—in all cases, you are driven to achieve. This means really looking at your career with the point of always wanting to achieve more of what you want.

Upward mobility often starts at the first stage of your career. Individuals I have worked with who are upwardly mobile come from all types of career fields: from the firefighter, to the IT worker, engineer, physician or CEO. While the objective may be different, the commonality is always the same: these individuals were always focused on moving up.

Upward Mobility has been the home of many Baby Boomers. The challenge that many of us encounter is that we are now finding ourselves in a different place in the career life cycle. What used to be motivating and fulfilling no longer "fits." We find it difficult to maintain the drive that has defined our careers to this point.

Even people in the early stages of their careers may find that moving up no long satisfies their needs and desires. It can be difficult to move away from the "upward mobility" career phase because sometimes we define ourselves by our most recent accomplishments. Stepping away from that may result in a significant "hit" to one's self image. This is a time when a good coach or mentor can help to reposition self image and newer, more relevant aspirations. Working through the Career Connection Quadrants in Chapter Four, *Finding Your Career Intersection of Skill and Passion,* can also be helpful in redefining the real intersection of your skills and passion.

Deceleration Position

The *Deceleration Position* can be exciting or it can be downright scary. This is a time in your career when you want to back off, have more personal time, or simply slow down. My experience has shown that it happens at least two or three times in a career. The first is when you decide you want to start a family, adopt a child, or maybe merge two families.

When this happens, it's common to want more time away from work with your new family, child, or relationship. Perhaps you no longer want to work the 80 hour weeks that you've thrived on; you want to devote the time to your child or children in building your family now. You may decide to go down one or two steps in the organization, or to work fewer hours, maybe even moving to part-time. You make a conscious decision to *decelerate* your career.

I personally went through a short-term career deceleration. It happened to me when my mom was diagnosed with lung cancer and congestive heart failure. We knew she had just three to six months to live. I approached my boss and shared what was happening in my life. Not only the situation and my need to be in another state with her for weeks to months, but also a well thought out plan for how I could do my job remotely. Thanks to some amazing co-workers, teleconferences and email, I was able to decelerate for the few weeks of her life and be there with her full time. It was an amazing gift—I was able to spend important time with my mom and my siblings, and still maintain a strong connection to work. That month became a transitional event—a cathartic "aha"—that changed my personal *and* professional life.

My story points out a critical component of successful deceleration. You need to have a plan to stay relevant, connected and vital to your job and your company. This is extremely important for those who leave the organization temporarily.

An interesting example is the "mommy track" which, in many households, has now become the "daddy track." Leaving to have a child, start a family, care for a family member or even just take off for a sabbatical can be a difficult disruption in anyone's career path. A lot can happen to disassociate yourself from colleagues, technology, even a change in a corporate culture, in just a few months. Re-entry to the business or corporate world is infinitely easier if you plan for your deceleration departure and return. You may even be able to—need to—negotiate your re-entry before you leave … not upon your return.

Lateral Movement

The *Lateral Movement* in your career positions you in one of "comfort" in terms of level. You are perfectly happy at your current level; you do not want to move up yet. You don't necessarily want more responsibility or more money. You might just say, "I'm in sales but I'd really like to move into marketing."

You are not asking for more of something other than an expanded experience, moving laterally in a company, hopefully doing something else that will enhance and enrich your background. The added benefit: It can be a great step to ultimately moving up in many companies. A lateral move can re-position you for a leap within the organization. One of the best things for your resume can be to show expertise in a variety of areas.

Outward Exit

Outward Exit can mean a number of different things. You may be at a point in your career where you are working for a manager that you don't enjoy working for or don't get along with. Do you decide to exit the company, or could you exit the department? Moving to another area within the organization under another supervisor can be a good move as an *Outward Exit*.

On the other hand, you may like your manager, and even the company, yet know you need to get out of the industry. It no longer feeds your soul or provides satisfaction. This may happen at the mid-career point where you have been in the same career for a number of years and need to change, or in a new career after moving into a new industry.

A good friend of mine held a high-level position at one of the best known beer companies. Over coffee one day, she shared with me, "I don't think the legacy I want to leave is selling beer." For her, she was right. What she decided to do was to leave her industry totally. Today, she owns her own business and is a sought-after executive coach. My friend *Exited Out*. At the end of the day a change in management, the culture, ownership—or even products—may result in a shift in your career satisfaction. For whatever reason, it is no longer a fit for you, and it might be time to exit out. Career management is discussed later in this book and provides some additional considerations to work through before leaving your present position, job, company or industry.

Enriching or Enhancing the Present

The *Enriching or Enhancing the Present* is (or may be) last on the list and can be the best place to be. Why? It's the place you love ... you love what you do ... you love where you work. And, you have no desire to change or leave. It doesn't matter if you are the CEO, the sales executive or the janitor. It's your spot. Think of star athletes; they do what they love and have no desire to do anything else.

Enriching or *Enhancing the Present* can also mean that you have found your niche where you just want to be the best you can possibly be—no matter what it is. Think of it as the sweet spot of your career; nothing can, or could, be better. Enjoy this position; it may last months, years, decades or forever.

It's Your Turn

Consider each of the five career positions. Make some notes on each position as to whether it resonates with you now. You may find some positions you recognize having been in at some time in your career. Note what that position was and what triggers caused you to move from that experience to another place on the map. All of these moves are transition points, and all tell you something about the triggers that cause you to make shifts in your career.

Upward Mobility

Deceleration

Lateral Movement

Outward Exit

Enriching or Enhancing the Present

Transition Point

Few of us actually create a career map. Some get lost, or don't know they are lost; some just wander around; some just plow ahead, never even thinking about it; some just coat tail onto someone else's "career map," not really conscious of what they are doing. Even others are directed by another's career choice for them. But, it is your career path; it is not someone else's.

It's not unusual to be in limbo during your working years. It is the case for many of my clients but can be detrimental to their careers. Knowing where you are, right now, allows you to determine where you want to go. Understanding where you are is the first step to determining if this is where you belong, or if you want to make a transition.

What Do You Want?

CHAPTER 3

Destiny is no matter of chance. It is a matter of choice.
It is not a thing to be waited for, it is a thing to be achieved.
—William Jennings Bryan

Sandy's Story

Sandy was a recent graduate from a highly acclaimed nursing school and while many openings came her way, for some reason, none appealed to her. She didn't know why, but she was hesitating to accept her first position. She turned down some opportunities because they required travel and one because the hospital was so large she felt like she would be lost in the crowd. One opportunity was attractive, but she would enter at the very bottom of the nursing staff and have zero control of her time, often being on call for multiple twenty-four hour shifts each month.

As we talked about her situation, Sandy was able to articulate a lot of reasons she didn't want to work for an organization, but she was not able to define what she was really looking for. As we worked through the process I will reveal next, she needed to get in touch with what really motivated her. What was it that gave her the "juice" she was looking for?

I went through nursing school because I like making people better. I want to know that I make a difference. I don't want to work for one of those hospitals that treat patients like cattle with little time to pay attention to them or their problems. And, I want to have some control over the hours I work; I don't want to be at the bottom of the pile and have to be on call so much that I can't have a life. I know I am asking for a lot, especially being a new nurse.

As we worked through and prioritized what was really important to her, she came to the realization that while she lived in a major city, she didn't necessarily need to stay there. She was mobile and wouldn't mind relocating. Sandy recognized that status was low on her list of priorities but patient care was high, and it was important that she get to know the people she was caring for. Further, she got back in touch with her love for the outdoors, and Sandy wanted to live in a place where she could camp, hike and go parasailing.

YES! I want to subscribe to **PEOPLE** and save!

- ☐ **54 WEEKLY ISSUES** at $1.86 each
  plus 23¢ postage and handling per issue
  — *PLUS 4 FREE ISSUES, for a total of 58!*

- ☐ **26 WEEKLY ISSUES** at $1.96 each
  plus 23¢ postage and handling per issue
  — *Save 54% off cover price!*

- ☐ Bill me later in full.
- ☐ Bill me later in 4 easy installments.

For faster service, go to people.com/get4free or call 1-866-353-2920

NAME _____ (PLEASE PRINT)

ADDRESS _____ APT. #_____

CITY _____ STATE ____ ZIP _____

E-MAIL _____ PEDL0T8

Plus sales tax where applicable. PEOPLE publishes 2 double issues. Each counts as 2 of 53 issues in an annual subscription. PEOPLE may also publish occasional extra issues. Offer good in U.S. only. Your first issue will mail 1-3 weeks from receipt of order.

16IPEIAG

Subscribe today for the Guaranteed Low Rate!

Order now at:
people.com/get4free

BUSINESS REPLY MAIL
FIRST-CLASS MAIL   PERMIT NO. 22   TAMPA FL

POSTAGE WILL BE PAID BY ADDRESSEE

People®

PO BOX 62120
TAMPA FL 33663-1201

NO POSTAGE
NECESSARY
IF MAILED
IN THE
UNITED STATES

When she completed her list of priorities and defined the things she would not compromise, the profile of jobs she would most like matched those of a smaller community located in an area of the country that had both wilderness for camping and hills for climbing.

Sandy shifted her search to an entirely different geography and ended up landing in a community hospital with a smaller staff, where she was instantly more senior because of her excellent academic credentials and clinical skills with the latest instruments and techniques. The values of the hospital were faith-based and focused entirely on the patient. Because the community was smaller, she got to know her patients and would even run into them at the local shopping area. Sandy had found her place—a place where she felt she was a true part of the community.

Starting a career can be a daunting experience. There are a lot of options before you and it can be tempting to jump at the first offer. Being clear about your priorities and what is really important can start you off in an area or location you may never have considered, but will meet many of your highest desires—as a result, it almost doesn't feel like work! Discovering and getting in touch with your own priorities is crucial in career success. Read on ...

What Do You Want?

Once you decide where you are in your career, your next task is to consider what you really want from your career. Think of your career as an open vessel. Your goal is to fill it. Why? Simply this: you need to allow your career to give you what you need.

In this chapter, you will learn the process to achieve this, a process that I have fine-tuned over a 15 year span. It's straightforward but important to understand; it will help you to identify, embrace and get what you *really want* from your career.

- ✦ Has your career given you anything more than a way to pay bills?
- ✦ Has your career just been a series of jobs with no objectives or real goals?
- ✦ Has it been a long time since you even thought about what *you* want?

This chapter will help you determine what is most important to you in your career.

Priority One: The Deal Breaker

Look at the most important attributes of your career. It's not going to be one thing; most likely there will be at least three key elements. What are the *must haves* of your career?

Take Gabe, an avid mountain climber. Evaluating the *must haves* for his career, he knew that living in a geographic area close to mountains was at the top of the list. Luckily, he lived in Boulder, Colorado, a location with great access to the mountains within a short distance from his home. Problem solved. But if he lived in a place lacking such access, moving to a geographically acceptable location would have been a serious possibility. For Gabe, it meant that he could easily schedule a morning or afternoon dedicated to mountain climbing without making it a major planning event.

This issue is not trivial. Gabe's work allowed him to work from his home office as a software technician. Managing his own time was paramount for his creative juices. Gabe's being in close proximity to a mountain environment actually fueled how he worked—it meant that he worked better, smarter, and more creatively. Along with flexible work conditions, he also wanted a career that would allow him to take frequent vacations ... another *must have*. Why? The lure of more distant challenging climbing goals require more than a weekend outing.

It might seem impossible to find a job and ultimately a career that allows you to work at home (during the hours you choose) and go away for two or three weeks at a time. Yet, it's not impossible—impossible becomes possible when it is generated from *negotiating*, sometimes with another individual—sometimes with yourself.

Gabe actually *negotiated* for the *must haves*. Getting more flexible time meant that he made a little bit less money, but money wasn't at the top of his list. It was not the most important thing to him. He was clear about the importance of money in his list of *must haves;* he also knew what his bottom line would be.

Must haves, among a variety of other items or issues, may include salary, position, title, geographic location or culture of an organization. Some individuals that I have worked with have reached a point in their careers where they want—and may need—to be close to aging parents. I've also seen people who have made career decisions based on the title they want.

One of my clients was President and COO of a major public company but his aspiration was to be CEO—within his own timeline. Although Tim was the heir apparent for the CEO role, the existing CEO was not ready to move on, so Tim actually resigned to follow his goal. He is now CEO of a fast growing, highly visible public company that also meets Tim's need to lead a company that makes a true difference in the world. Whether your priority is a title, role, salary or location, be clear and focused and build your career plan to achieve it.

> It is important to be crystal clear about your *must haves* ... the ones that are really *non-negotiable for you*. If you don't receive them or already have them, then the job is off the table and is not to be considered.

Priority Two: The Icing on the Cake

Next, define those attributes that are desirable but fall farther down on your priority list. It is important to recognize these attributes that are not deal breakers, but would still be nice to have; mention them, because often organizations will offer these up as negotiating tools. *Don't let them be deal breakers.* Rather, think of them as possible perks—not critical, just nice to have.

Think of the time when you were a kid at the ice cream counter with all 31 flavors in front of you. When you walked in, you knew you wanted a double scoop of vanilla, but now surrounded by 30 other flavors with fantastic names attached to them, you are much less certain. Be clear on *The Deal Breakers*, what items would be the *Icing on the Cake* and what belongs in *The Goodie Bag* (coming up next).

Identify the things that would be great to have. Not critical, but terrific perks to your overall career. These are possible *adders*.

For example, you may consider the following:

✦ It would be nice to live in a place that has four seasons; or,

- ✦ It would be great to work in a place with tuition aid, in case I go back to school; or,
- ✦ It would be ideal to have a worksite that has on-site day care. It's not a deal breaker for me, but it sure would be nice.

These *adders* are items that may make your work easier, add convenience to your overall workload or provide something "extra," but they are really not necessary.

Priority Three: The Goodie Bag

At the end of the day, you have gotten your *must haves* and your *adders* within a couple of opportunities. *The Goodie Bag* becomes the final differentiator. None are critical to you or the work you do ... but would be a nice "goodie" to have. Things like a gym membership, discounts to the local golf course, season tickets to your favorite sport, an affinity club or the use of company baseball seats a few times during the season. (Keep in mind, these items could be on your *must have* list even though they are low priority on somebody else's.)

For most companies, *The Goodie Bag* includes items that are not costly but potentially attractive to a candidate. Companies think of them as "throw-aways."

Beware! If you are not clear about your priorities, you may be overwhelmed by the number of extras—*The Goodie Bag*—an organization is offering you, when in reality they are not the attributes that are really most important to you.

It's Your Turn

Identify your Deal Breakers, Icing on the Cake and Goodie Bag components in the space below as a starter. You might want to take a visual twist to it and use sticky notes or post on a flip chart or white board so they stay out in front of you at all times. Or, create a section on your desktop that you can quickly access as a reminder when you are talking with anyone about you and your career.

Priority One:
The Deal Breaker. **What are your *Must Haves*?**

_____

_____

_____

_____

_____

_____

_____

_____

_____

Priority Two:
Icing on the Cake. What are your "It would be *Great to Haves*"?

_____

_____

_____

_____

_____

_____

_____

_____

_____

_____

Priority Three:
The Goodie Bag. What are your "It would be *Fun or Nice to Haves*"?

_____
_____
_____
_____
_____
_____
_____
_____
_____
_____

Transition Point

It is impossible to mentally and physically move forward without knowing where you are, where you want to go and why you want to get there.

It is your "come to career" moment.

Finding Your Career Intersection of Skill and Passion

CHAPTER 4

Choose a job you love, and you will never have to work a day in your life.
—Confucius

Mary's Story

Mary lost her job as a human resources manager at a large tech organization and was provided career transition services to help her move on to her next position. In the beginning she revised her resume and began networking and connecting to new people and organizations to find a job.

When we met, Mary shared that after looking for four months, she was frustrated and was having a hard time maintaining her focus and energy. As we discussed her past role, it was evident that she had a wide and deep background in many areas of human resources. With her experience, she was definitely qualified for a number of generalist positions that I knew were available in the market at that time.

> Yes, I have had a couple of offers but they were for things that I don't really want to do anymore. It's hard because they are attracted to areas in my background covering compensation and benefits. I have done it, and I have done it well but truth be known, I hated doing it.

This revelation was important for Mary, so I asked her to make a list of all the roles she had already held and to break each down to the core areas of responsibility. Mary worked on the list for a couple of weeks and came back to meet with me with a long and detailed inventory of her areas of expertise.
"This is an impressive list, Mary. Based on my knowledge of the market today, you should have had multiple offers by now."

> Like we talked before, I have had a couple, but one was going to make me a manager in compensation and benefits. That is one of the areas of HR that I really find boring, so I turned it down. The other one was a human resources generalist but as I looked at the job description and talked to the hiring manager, I felt like it would be a step back. At this point in my career

I just don't feel like I should have to do that, so I said no to that one too. My list is exhaustive but there is a lot on here that I don't want to ever do again, but it seems like they are the areas that companies find the most attractive about my background.

Mary had been working for a number of years in a field that she had largely mastered. Based on her great expertise, she was also compensated well and often got awards for her accomplishments. I asked her why she had stayed in those roles for so long if she didn't like them.

I kept getting bonuses and promotions and every time I suggested a change to a different role, my bosses would tell me I was too valuable and they would not support me in moving. It was nice to get the constant recognition, but even that didn't do it for me anymore. And now that I lost that job, I don't want to be stuck in a similar rut again.

I presented the four quadrants to Mary and explained that when I meet anyone who feels stuck and de-energized, I usually find that they are working in areas and at roles that they are very good at, but have either lost the love for, or never had it in the first place.

It is difficult to move from those roles if you do get accolades and compensation that handcuff you, since that part feels good. As we walked through the quadrants, Mary frowned as she recognized that much of what she had been doing sat on the side of *good at, but don't love*.

> This is really depressing! I feel like I have wasted the past seven years of my career. Why didn't I do something about this sooner?

Mary moved each of the items from her list to the quadrant they best fit into, and while the vast majority was on the energy draining side of things she was good at but didn't really like, a small but promising list did emerge on the side of things she really did enjoy—had some passion about. As we looked at the four completed quadrants, I asked Mary to concentrate on the right side of the model, focusing on the things that she was really passionate about and also had a good deal of skill.

> I see what I like and what I am really good at, but what kind of job can I get with that list? It doesn't look like a job to me.

We spent some time talking about the patterns in what she loved, and then brainstormed about career options that might match. When Mary said the words,

> I guess my favorite part of my past jobs was really doing the coaching and mentoring of my teams. I do get a lot of energy when I think about

all of those people, and some of them still come back to meet with me even today.

Yes, she realized what her new career was. Being a coach would be an ideal fit for her.

Mary began to focus on companies that supported coaching roles for human resource professionals as a bona fide position. Once she narrowed down what she really wanted, it became clear which companies might fit the bill. It took her several more months to land her job and at the end of the day, she felt it was worth the wait.

For the first time in so long, I feel excited about my job; I actually look forward to coming to work every day. The company also seems to really value the work I am doing with the team, and the people I have met with have been so appreciative.

Mary's journey of discovery took some time, but with the clarity she gained around what she loves and is good at, she will likely not end up 'wasting' time again or feeling stuck. The quadrant work that she went through revealed her pathway.

What comes next is a dynamic process of making sure you are maximizing your time and your talents, and always feeling good!

Finding Your Career Intersection of Skill and Passion

This chapter is all about getting clear about your skills, talents and abilities, and, most importantly, your passion. Once you understand the intersection of your skills and passion, you have found your sweet spot! This is seriously nirvana: energy producing, joyous enthusiasm. This is where you want to spend time in your job or career.

Step 1: Inventory Your Skills, Talents, Abilities and Experiences

The list you make will be of all the things you have done or know how to do. This list is not just about your job or career experiences, it is a major "dump" of all the things you can think of that you have done or know how to do. Let me give you an example.

Liz had been a project manager for several years, so her list of skills and experiences included:

- ✦ Create project plans
- ✦ Input and manage Visio software program
- ✦ Schedule team meetings

- Build milestones for team accountability
- Track all milestone activity and follow up
- Etc. (she had many more)

Through our discussions, Mary began to list several more skills that she didn't routinely think about, something that I find more common than not. I then asked Mary to consider other things she had done in her life. Her eyes lit up and she shared that she had managed a Girl Scout troop for her daughter. I asked her to tell me what that entailed. She shared,

> We all had so much fun. My favorite part was organizing events for the annual cookie sale. We created different ways to help the girls sell; in fact, we as Scout leaders actually sold too!

As she continued on to tell me how her teams had surpassed all goals and won multiple awards, it was obvious that she not only had other skills but other passions as well. These are just a few of the additional skills Mary was able to add to her list:

- Create and staff events
- Design sales contests
- Sell
- Motivate teams
- Etc.

She had many more; in fact, several dozen more. Had we not specifically delved further into Mary's "other life," we never would have built an exhaustive list from which to build her next career. Mary's love for staging events, managing the process and creative selling actually ended up leading her to the work she loves today as a successful event planner! We will talk more later about how "shaping an entirely new career" can be accomplished, leveraging skills and background you already have.

So, back to the list—*your* list. Make it as comprehensive as possible. When I first did this, I actually had my kitchen lined with flip chart pages so that every time I walked by and remembered another skill or experience I had, I could immediately add it to my list.

> **Your inventory of skills, experiences and talents should not be limited to your current or past jobs. Consider EVERYTHING you can think of and add it to the list—even if it was something you didn't like doing or were never very good at.**

If you are a visual person, like me, you can build your list on huge flip chart pages and line your office, kitchen or living room walls. However, you may be a bit more discrete. So go ahead and type it into your computer, or build the list in your journal.

Just Build It!

It's Your Turn

Inventory

- ✦ Write down all your current job or career duties (easily done by pulling from your current or recent job description).
- ✦ Capture skills and experiences from past jobs (if you don't have a job description go to the net and look at similar jobs).
- ✦ Include experiences, skills and talents from your life, not just your jobs.
- ✦ If you are not in a job or have never had one, consider volunteer work you've done, team roles you've had, or talents and abilities you discovered in school or from your parents and others in your life. For example, people may have told you how great you are at math, reading or spelling, etc.

_____
_____
_____
_____
_____
_____
_____
_____
_____
_____

- Once you have completed your "dump" list, you are ready to move on to the next step below.

Understand The Career Connection Quadrants Model

I started working on *The Career Connection Quadrants Model* more than a decade ago to help me understand what skills, talents and experience I had, and how or if they would play a role in my next career move. I recognized that while I knew how to do a lot of things, and I had a lot of experience, there were some things I really enjoyed and was good at, and some things that I may have been good at, but I really did not want to do again.

The Career Connection Quadrants Model is a great way to be clear about both what you are good at and what you really want to do in your next career move:

Quadrant I   *What I'm good at, but I do not love.*
Quadrant II   *What I'm not good at and don't love at all.*
Quadrant III *What I love, but I'm not good at yet.*
Quadrant IV   *What I love and I'm really good at.*

The Career Connection Quadrants

What I Am Good At

Quadrant I:
What I'm good at, but I do not love.

Quadrant IV:
What I love and I'm really good at.

Quadrant II:
What I'm not good at and don't love at all.

Quadrant III:
What I love, but I'm not good at yet.

What I Love

Quadrant I: Consists of things that you are good at or maybe even great at doing but you really *don't like* doing them. I have found that the skills in this quadrant are often the skills your mom and dad always told you "were your gift." These talents also sometimes have gotten us into the jobs we are now in. Some of these skills may even be invisible to you—you don't really think of them as "skills," you just do them. And let's face it, we all do things within our workplaces because we are there, it's part of our job and it needs to be done … and you are the one that somehow gets it done.

There may be an art gene that bubbles out—those PowerPoint graphics you add to the monthly sales presentation always get "wows" from your co-workers. But it's a grind! You don't love it, even though you are good to great at it.

It could also be sales—you might be good at sales and talented and able to make sales but you might really not like doing it. You could be an amazing number cruncher—there isn't a financial statement that you can't master. But truth be told, you are sick of numbers and the last thing you want to see is another financial statement or do another tax return. You've got the skills, yet you just don't love it.

These examples are clear candidates for Quadrant I: *What I'm good at, but I do not love.*

Quadrant II: The bottom left is the quadrant you want to avoid like the plague: *What I'm not good at and don't* *love at all*. You do things because you have to, or feel you have to do them. Each time you engage in one, you feel the negative pull. You may even start an ongoing inner dialogue, one that you've had multiple times, "I can't stand this … I can't wait until this is over … Why me?"

Why indeed. I'm notorious for telling my coaching clients this is the "Run, Forrest, Run" quadrant, from the movie *Forrest Gump*. In this quadrant, nobody wins and nobody is happy. You don't like doing these things and you are not good at them anyway. Get out, and the sooner the better for everyone. As a side note, I recognize that every job includes things—duties or responsibilities—that are not your "favorites," but also includes areas that are positive. It's the negatives that are making you miserable. In a later chapter, I'll share tips on how you can stay in a position, get more mileage out of what you enjoy doing, and delete, reduce or delegate the negatives that are adding to your misery zone at work.

Again, don't limit yourself; think outside of the workplace. If being the taxi driver for the neighborhood kids, attending three soccer games a week or having to create the evening meal, emptying the dishwasher, washing the car, anything around the house—you name it—is at the top of the list of not wanting to do, write it down. You are identifying anything that you are not good at and do not want to do again. They all belong in Quadrant II.

Quadrant III: This is what I call the "garden." This quadrant includes areas that you love or really like, but you've really never gotten good at them. What I generally find is the reason we're not good at these things is that we spend too much time in Quadrants I and II and then have no time to nurture and get better at the things we love.

Quadrant III is a garden because it's all those things that you really do enjoy doing but may never have had time to do. These are the kinds of things that are going to bubble up to Quadrant IV because the more you do them (which will be easy if you can find the time), the better you will become at them.

Quadrant IV: This is nirvana, the quadrant where we reside when we are doing what we love and are really good at. This is Peyton Manning's quadrant—he loves playing football. He's very, very good at it, and he really doesn't want to do anything else.

Often, people will say when they're in this quadrant, "I can't believe they pay me to do this!"

The next step in the process will be to take each line item from your list and plug it into the appropriate quadrant.

An abbreviated example from my personal *Career Connection Quadrants* visual looked like the next page after I entered all the entries from my list into the appropriate quadrants.

The Career Connection Quadrants

What I Am Good At ↑	**Quadrant I:** • Running a P&L for an organization • Managing people in teams • Creating PowerPoints and visuals • Preparing reports for investor road shows • Managing monthly budgets	**Quadrant IV:** • Public speaking • Presenting • Selling • Motivating/ inspiring teams and people • Coaching • Creating new solutions • Innovating
	Quadrant II: • Data compilation • Project management • Tracking monthly, weekly performance progress • Creating detailed spreadsheets • Following all the rules	**Quadrant III:** • Theater/acting • Baking • Managing Boards for organizations • Communicating with analysts in roadshows

What I Love →

It's Your Turn

Transfer to Four Quadrants

Once you get your list together of all the things you've done and everything that you know how to do, the next step is to transfer it to the *The Career Connection Quadrants Model*.

Take each item from your "dump" list and decide in which quadrant it belongs.

Move each item to one of the four quadrants (yes, they all belong somewhere!).

The Career Connection Quadrants

What I Am Good At

Quadrant I:

Quadrant IV:

Quadrant II:

Quadrant III:

What I Love

In looking at my own quadrants, there were several career options I could have considered:

- ✦ Sales/Business Development
- ✦ Public Speaker
- ✦ New Product Development Leader
- ✦ Innovation Leader
- ✦ Investor Relations Leader
- ✦ Counselor
- ✦ Coach

Where I ended up was doing what I'm good at and what I love. I started with Lee Hecht Harrison in Business Development and continued to follow my strengths and passions and am now a Senior Vice President with the ability to do coaching, public speaking and team leadership.

As I have used the *Four Quadrants* over the years, I have found that some of them change over time. I continually re-evaluate my own quadrants to ensure that I am spending my time primarily in Quadrants III and IV. If I find that I am spending too much time in Quadrants I and II, my body and work feels it, I am tired and much less productive. I can guarantee you that I am also experiencing more stress and less enjoyment and fulfillment when that is the case.

Always strive to spend your time in Quadrants III and IV.

Transition Point

Now that you have a sense of what you are good at and what you love doing, it is time to consider how to manage the *The Career Connection Quadrants*. That will depend upon your situation: Will you want to make a career change or just want to increase your fulfillment and satisfaction in your current career?

Everyone is a genius but if you judge a fish on its ability to climb a tree, it will live its whole life believing it is stupid.

—Albert Einstein

Making Choices in Your Career

CHAPTER 5

The only way to do great work is to love what you do. If you haven't found it yet, keep looking. Don't settle. As with all matters of the heart, you'll know when you find it.
—Steve Jobs

Joe's Story

When you work in any city, you become aware of the reputations of organizations, some are viewed as great places to work and some are viewed as pretty challenging; some you just don't go there. Joe worked for an organization that had a good reputation in the market so I was surprised when he asked to meet with me to discuss his dissatisfaction with his job and his company.

Joe had been at the organization for a little more than a year as a new college hire. He had been brought into the supply chain company and had high hopes for quick advancement. It was not happening. In fact, at his one year performance review he was rated at meeting expectations in some areas and missing expectations in team partnering and leadership. Joe was frustrated that he was not at the top of the promotion list; he was not even on a high potential list.

> I am not sure I fit with this company. I don't think they recognize what I bring to the table. I thought that the people at this company were the best in class, but in meetings I am amazed at how much they resist ideas that could make us more successful.

I asked Joe how he was doing with his own team. "Some of them are okay, but there are a lot of whiners. They complain about everything and I don't think they are willing to carry their own water. I'm not so sure that I want to lead a team if it is going to be like this. Now that I think about it, my team might even be holding me back from a promotion."

Joe was clearly disillusioned, and the fact that he observed that the organization was not doing anything about his frustration made him wonder if he was at the right company. As we talked further, I asked him to identify some specific situations where things were not going well. He quickly shared a couple of examples where his boss said he was not meeting expectations on a deliverable. Joe felt the root cause was that his boss had not clearly defined his expectations in the first place, so it was not his fault. These situations, no doubt, resulted in his overall performance rating.

I wrote the situations Joe shared on a white board and asked him what the outcome was for each. In both cases, it was an ugly confrontation. His boss walked away feeling that Joe was not delivering, and therefore, his overall performance rating was compromised. Then we discussed how Joe had responded to the situation. His response of arguing his point was the same with each confrontation. I asked him if his response (arguing) had gotten him the outcome he wanted, and not surprising, the answer was "No."

Joe blamed it on his boss' ineffective communication style and lack of clarity. Clearly, what Joe was doing was not working, so I asked him, "What could you do differently to get a different outcome?"

"Well, even though I shouldn't have to, I guess I could ask him for more clarity in what he wants when he assigns me a project."

That was a great start because it would likely change what Joe submitted in the end. We also talked about how Joe responded to his boss, including that it sounded like he was argumentative, angry, and his voice and mannerisms showed it. Joe agreed to try shifting his response the next time his boss assigned a deliverable.

I met with Joe a couple of weeks later. His boss had given him a new project with a short turnaround time. At the time of the request, Joe stopped before leaving and restated what he thought his boss had asked for. Not to my surprise, it turned out Joe's expectation was not the same as his boss'. His boss clarified what he was really looking for. When Joe completed the project, his boss complimented him not only on the quality of the project, but also told him that he really appreciated him asking for clarity on the scope of the deliverable.

"My boss finally seems to recognize that he doesn't communicate well" was Joe's summation. In reality, Joe changed how *he* responded to the situation, and in doing so, he actually impacted the outcome.

The relationship became stronger and over a six month period of time Joe had pulled himself out of the "not meeting expectations" category and according to his boss was on his way to the high potential list.

Joe used the same process to work through the dynamics of his own team. He found that by changing the way he was responding to the situation or person, he began to see positive changes in the outcomes he was getting. Joe, like most of us, initially attributed his new successes to *the other person finally changing*. But in reality, Joe was the person who changed and his response was the only thing he could really control. Joe now believes that the company is a better place to work, and is viewing his next step as a promotion instead of a walk out the door.

These situations happen regularly in organizations and it leads to unnecessary terminations, low morale and the loss of valuable talent. Throughout your career, you will have decisions to make in your career. The intent of this chapter is to be clear about what you are facing and how to make an intentional choice, rather than one out of fear, frustration or anger. By understanding the root of the issues faced, you can make a successful transition and move your career in the right direction.

Making Choices in Your Career

At this stage, you should now be more aware of where you are in your career from multiple perspectives. Let's talk about how you manage your career based on what you have learned.

As an Executive Coach, I often work with people who are frustrated or unhappy in their current role and believe that they need to leave the company; quit their job. That may well be the case, but first, it is important to evaluate exactly what causes the frustration or lack of fulfillment. Once the cause is understood, you can determine the best next steps.

When frustrated, it may seem your only choice is to leave the organization—the sooner, the better. Yet, is that the best solution? Here's what I tell my coaching clients, and it's exactly what you, my reader, need to hear at this point:

> It is never an easy choice to leave an organization. Your best bet to deal with dissatisfaction initially is to see if there is something you can do to make the job more enjoyable. Even if you have to leave, it is much easier to find a job when you have a job.

Having said that, I fully recognize that sometimes it is time to leave; that may indeed be the best choice. A couple of years ago I worked with a high-level leader from a major corporation. She reported directly to the CEO and was frustrated and tired of her role, tired enough that she was ready to leave. Through some processing and discussion, we determined that Angela was on the edge of total exhaustion; she had worked herself into a frenzy. In such a situation it is not wise to make a career changing decision. We decided that she needed to rejuvenate and recharge. Angela took a few weeks off during that summer and spent some time with her family, considering and exploring what she really wanted.

At the end of that summer, we met again, and now, rested and thinking more clearly, Angela understood that she was frustrated with her boss, but she also had not been stepping forward to clearly state her expectations and desire to enrich her career. Before taking the time off and finding enough space to really reconnect with herself, she didn't even know what she truly wanted. Angela ultimately clarified her career "sweet spot" and was able to present a plan to her CEO that both met her needs and desires and those of the corporation. Angela also discovered that she wanted to become a mentor and role model for women in the organization.

Two years later, happy in her career direction, she received the Woman of the Year award by the Women's Vision Foundation. Spending time to come to a quality decision paid off for both Angela and her organization in many ways.

Choices—Always a Good Thing

Career Situation #1:
I don't think I want to leave or change careers, but I want more satisfaction.

For one thing, you are not alone. The club you are in is the "I'm unhappy in my job" club, and your co-members include more than 75 percent of the population. If that's your position in a current role or job, and you have completed your priorities and quadrants, you have most likely identified too many items that fall into Quadrants I and II and possibly too few in Quadrants III and IV.

You have several preliminary options to consider:

1. Figure out how to move items from Quadrants I and II to Quadrants III or IV; i.e., understand what you dislike and see if you can make some parts more enjoyable.
2. Get rid of the tasks in Quadrants I and II:
    a. Delegate them out; or,
    b. Just stop doing them—if that's possible.
    Sometimes you never know until you try!

As you evaluate what are in Quadrants I and II, here are some questions to ask yourself:

✦ Is it the task or responsibility I dislike, or is it the person or team?
✦ Have I ever liked doing this in the past, and, if *yes*, what has changed?

- How often do I have to do this task or have this responsibility?
- Who or what requires this task to be done?
- Are there components of the task that I do like?
- Is this task critical to what I do?

As you ask these questions, you will begin to understand the root cause of the discomfort or frustration.

When It Is the Task Itself that Leads to Frustration

You may have processed through the questions above and come to the conclusion that the tasks are the issue. If it is not the people, then you can construct strategies to either eliminate the tasks or find ways to make them less frustrating and, if at all possible, more enjoyable.

The first thing to do is to determine what tasks or parts of tasks can be delegated or stopped. Below are a variety of ways to manage the frustrating or unappealing tasks:

- **Evaluate and Tweak:** Look at the task in terms of its components. How might you restructure the task to minimize the unappealing aspects? Is it the task itself, or the timing of the task that bothers you? Expense reports are a great example. They usually are due once per month and within a certain timeframe. Waiting until the last minute, the task can seem overwhelming and a frustration trigger for you.

One suggestion to relieve the pressure of something like expense reports noted above is to break the task down into components. Allocate a few minutes each day to add new items to your report. By the end of the month, the task may not seem so overwhelming or distasteful—in fact, the final report may be merely glanced over to make sure nothing has been omitted or needs correction.

✦ **Delegate or Trade:** Look at each of your tasks or duties in Quadrant I and/or II. Would someone else enjoy these tasks? If you are the leader of a team, look at creating a development opportunity for a team member. Why don't you give a team member some of the tasks you dislike, or are not good at? If you are not a team leader, check with your teammates to see if there are tasks you could trade with them.

They may have tasks in their Quadrant I and/or II that are in your Quadrant III or IV. Once you both agree, you may have to get approval from your boss, but usually if you are proactive and the work will assuredly be done, the boss can be convinced.

This strategy is surprisingly successful. Most don't think about it or view it as an option. It's not unusual for a boss to view this as a very proactive attitude within the team.

- **Confirm the Necessity of the Task:** Ask your boss or the person requesting the information, report, or task this one question: Is it still important? Often tasks remain active long after they are necessary, but everyone assumes they still must be done. You may find that the task is obsolete and is long past its expiration date.
- **Stop Doing the Task:** This can be a risky strategy. You need to be confident enough to acknowledge the risk and possible consequences. On the other hand, you may find that no one misses it when you stop doing it. Evaluate the risk!

When the People, Team or Boss Are at the Root of the Frustration

If you continue to come back to the fact that the team or individuals (even the boss) are the root cause of frustration and not the task, you have a different set of questions to consider:

- How would I articulate the issues I have with the individual, team or boss?
- Have I discussed my frustrations with the other members of the team or my boss?

If you have not had a conversation with the "offending individuals," this is a natural starting point. As a responsible individual, leader or team member, it is your responsibility to go directly to the individuals with your concerns, questions or frustrations. Put your "big boy or girl" pants on and talk to them. Yes, this is your responsibility, and remember you are doing this not for them—but to get you what you want.

Hopefully, such a conversation will clarify the situation, allowing alleviation of some of your concerns. If you are worried about how to have such a conversation, talk to a coach or read a book such as *Crucial Conversations* by Patterson, Grenny, McMillan and Switzler. Either can give you some pointers on how best to handle the situation.

We often think that we could get along with people if only they would behave in a different way. But you can't control what other people do. The model that I've used successfully for years is adaptable in a variety of different situations. The algorithm is:

$$E + R \rightarrow O$$

Here is how it works.

The E stands for events that happen. Let's face it, things happen all the time in our lives and include things like the furnace goes out, your car dies, or someone does something that bugs you.

The R in the algorithm is your response to that event. The next thing that happens is you respond to that event.

You may respond in a lot of different ways: you may get angry, you may kick your car tire, you may yell at another person. Or, you may decide to share your expansive vocabulary with anyone and everyone.

The O in the algorithm is the ultimate outcome. The most important thing to remember is this:

The way you Respond to an event or person drives the Outcome.

Many think in the E + R = O algorithm. Wrong! Event plus Response doesn't just equal Outcome. Don't go there. *Event plus Response fundamentally DRIVES Outcome.* Thus, the $E + R \to O$ *model* is far more powerful in recognizing the impact—and ownership—that *you* have of the Outcome created.

Let me give you an example. John was a very busy and successful executive, always rushing to get to appointments, checking his voicemail in the car and sometimes even doing his email along the way. (I don't recommend any of this.) One morning on his way to work, he was running late as usual, driving fast, passing every car in his way. Another driver tried to pass John. John was so irritated that he sped up to stop the person from getting ahead of him (because, of course, nothing was going to get in his way that morning).

The other driver still merged to get in front of him, so he sped up again—this time he hit the other car. When the two drivers got out of their cars, John was livid, "How could you be so stupid, you just caused an accident!" The other driver looked at John, "What do you mean *I am stupid* ... You hit *me*."

The outcome for John was not so great. He was cited for the accident, now had a damaged car, was late for his meeting, and his insurance went up due to the accident ... and his impatience. When we talked, John still thought it was the other driver's fault. He was blaming the outcome (his inconvenience and damage) on the event (the accident) when in reality had he responded in a different way, he *never* would have caused the accident in the first place.

Working with him and walking through the $E + R \rightarrow O$ model, I asked John, "How might you have responded differently to the other driver?" He finally admitted that he was entirely responsible for the outcome. It was a moment of realization. It's a major transitional moment when you learn to *own* your response and your contribution to the outcome.

The secret to this simple algorithm that I have used for more than 15 years, and most likely, has been around for over one hundred years is:

The only piece of this equation that you control is your response to what happens. Always.

It is as consistent and reliable as any law of physics: you can choose how you respond to any event or to anyone's behavior. *Always.* In your career (and in your life), one of the most important things to understand is that the one thing you *always* can control is how you respond to any event that happens. People will tell me years after they learned this model that "it still works!"—yeah, like any law of physics.

> **As long as you blame outcomes on events or other people, you make yourself a victim.**

Victims in life always look at the outcome and blame the event that caused it, when in reality had they changed the way they responded to that event, they literally could have changed the outcome.

The $E + R \rightarrow O$ *model* is a powerful but simple truth. What you want to understand is that to resolve some of the issues you have with other people, and yourself, you need to stop focusing on what they are doing and start looking at how you might change the way you are responding to them.

Think about the things that people do that trigger problems in your relationship with them. Then think about what you could do differently in response to what they do.

> **Always remember that by changing how you respond to an event or an individual, you will change the outcome.**

Another side of $E + R \rightarrow O$ *model* is something, often quoted, that Einstein said: "If you keep doing what you are doing, you will keep getting what you are getting." The original definition of insanity.

> **The bottom line: if something or someone is triggering a response in you that keeps leading to an outcome you don't want, change the way you respond. That is the only thing you can control 100 percent of the time.**

Sometimes, however, your best attempts to resolve the issues just don't work, and you continue to feel frustrated and dissatisfied. If this turns out to be the case, you have another set of questions to consider:

- ✦ Is there any other team I could move to within the organization?
- ✦ Is there another leader I could transfer to?
- ✦ What would it take to keep me at this company?
- ✦ What would it take to make me leave this company?

Depending upon the answers to these questions you may need to consider re-evaluating your place in the five career positions and think about exiting or making a lateral move within the company. If you have a good HR department or business partner you can confide in, they may be able to assist you in defining possible options. Once again, this is also where a good coach can assist you in defining and evaluating next steps.

Career Situation #2:
I am looking for my perfect job.

As an Executive Coach, I am frequently asked to assist people in finding their perfect job or career. If you are thinking about a new job or a new career, the most important thing to understand is that you want a role that allows you to work primarily in Quadrants III and IV—remember, these are your sweet spots.

Several years ago, I was working with a very senior level leader who held what was the equivalent of a General Manager role and next in line for the CEO role. As we progressed through our coaching, I became concerned about whether or not he really wanted to stay on his current path of succession.

I pulled together a list of the key competencies and expectations of a CEO. Without telling him exactly what it was, I asked him to go through the list and select everything that he would put in his Quadrants III and IV. As you might guess, he selected very few items on the list.

This was an eye-opening experience. In doing this brief, yet significant exercise, he realized that this was not a role he would find fulfilling. He declined the role and continued doing work that he found even more satisfying—the work he was already doing as the GM! A few years later, I asked him if it had been a difficult decision to step away and whether he felt he had made the right choice. His response:

> If I had not been working through *The Career Connection Quadrants* and become so aware of my true desires, I would have taken the new role and been miserable. Although it was difficult at the time to say 'no' to what I thought I had always been working toward, I have no regrets.

As you review potential openings, whether that be through job descriptions or meeting with recruiters or potential new employers, review the list of expectations that the potential employer provides. Ask questions about the most critical functions and objectives. Now that you are aware of items that you dislike or don't want to engage in, clearly you should avoid positions that have a number of those activities or duties in your Quadrants I and II. It is inevitable that the position includes some of those aspects (as most positions will). If you feel that enough falls into your Quadrants III and IV, then the pros sufficiently outweigh the cons. You may take the position, but make sure you refer back to the previous discussion on how to mitigate the distasteful tasks or expectations.

There are many great resources available (including excellent coaches) to assist you in making a successful assimilation into the new role.

It's Your Turn

Identify a challenge you have in your current role, and define it as a person, team or task.

_____
_____
_____
_____
_____
_____
_____
_____
_____
_____

Write down how you have responded to the challenge, and acknowledge at the end—is it working for you?

What could you do differently?

Transition Point

Regardless of where you are in your career—making a change or enhancing your current role—it is your responsibility to own your choices and how you respond to any resulting event or situation. Always remember, you do have significant control over the outcomes because you choose the response.

$$E + R \rightarrow O$$
(Events + Response → Outcome)

Managing Your Career

CHAPTER 6

Whatever you can do, or dream you can, begin it ...
Boldness has genius, power, and magic in it.
—Goethe

Bill's Story

It takes energy, focus and drive to make it to the top of sales in a well-known public company. Bill had been there four years, hired shortly out of college, promoted to Regional Sales Manager and was eyeing the Areas Sales Director role. The company was growing fast enough to justify adding a new Director, which meant that he didn't have to wait for someone to retire to be considered.

Bill had always been a top sales producer and when he was promoted to Regional Manager, it was the first time he had a team of direct reports. He had been in the role for eighteen months, and his first performance appraisal had been after six months on the new job. Bill came to see me after his second performance review had just been completed.

> I can't believe what just happened. Not only am I not on the list for the new Director role, I am on some ridiculous performance plan. This makes no sense, my sales results are the best of any of the Regional Sales Managers.

As we talked about the feedback he received, Bill shared that while he had strong sales results, he also had the highest turnover of any of the managers, and his one year 360 indicated some serious relationship issues with his peers.

> Of course my peer group doesn't 'like' me—we are all sales leaders, and we're competitive. I am beating their results hands down—what else are they going to say? They pay me to get results and I do just that. Yes, some of my team has left, the ones who couldn't hack it. I drive myself hard and I drive them hard, too. It's the only way to get results—if they don't like it, I invite them to leave.

Bill was contemplating leaving the company, his patience was ebbing and he felt he deserved the promotion based on his results. While leaving was certainly one of his options, I asked him what would be different at the next company. Bill was a natural born sales guy, he was competitive and he was driven to achieve results. Many sales people have a unique working challenge; they are top in their field but it's because they operate alone; they learn that they can depend upon their own abilities—rarely needing much assistance from others. In coaching, I am always cautious when discussing their career aspirations, while many are upwardly mobile, they don't necessarily thrive in leading others. When evaluating their intersection of skill and passion, it is often the case that what they love is the act of closing the deal, driving to higher and higher results, and being richly rewarded for just that behavior.

Bill was an exception in that he did enjoy leading teams to achieve results, he liked the power and status of the role and he liked directing outcomes; so it wasn't that he was operating in an area of low passion but his skill level was not developed. He also did not have a strong network of support in the company, and his understanding of "how to get along" in the company culture at his new level was missing. Finally, Bill was strong at the control factor of leading a team, but he was not actually using his influence to get things done. This created strife between him and his direct reports and even his peers; people would choose to leave instead of submitting to his leadership.

Upward mobility was Bill's chosen path, he wanted to manage larger teams and have a greater impact on the future of the company than he could through his own sales efforts alone. We also talked about his commitment to this particular company. He had originally been drawn to the mission and vision of the organization, and the culture was one of the few fast enough moving to satisfy his desire to move up.

Using Bill's 360 data and some of the exit data from his past employees we started to identify areas he could focus on to achieve his objectives. I also did some interviews with stakeholders who could impact Bill's chances for success. One of the results of Bill's proactive work to address the areas identified for development was that his boss and key stakeholders took a greater interest in his career aspirations; they were impressed that he would commit to following through on the areas defined. This level of buy-in is almost impossible to garner without taking decisive action. Bill stepped up to the challenge and bought a lot of credibility along the way.

Managing a team for the first time is a challenge, very different from driving individual results. Bill had to figure out how working through and with his team would benefit him and lead to higher results. However, in addition to understanding some of the bottom line impacts, it was also very important for Bill to *want* to have stronger relationships; he didn't enjoy his lack of relationships with his team and his peers. As a "people person", he needed to acknowledge that he would get greater satisfaction if he could have stronger relationships. Just as Bill had previously focused on driving sales numbers, he now needed to expand his competitive nature to work at retaining high quality talent, a different kind of goal. Based on his sales expertise, he clearly had the ability to create and maintain relationships, so developing relationships with his direct reports was not overly difficult; it just required a different perspective. Bill was not insincere about these relationships, he genuinely enjoyed people and when he refocused his attention, his team responded well and his turnover rate began to fall.

As Bill continued to focus his attention on building relationships (with his peers as well as his direct reports) he noticed that he had greater influence on creating outcomes. He found that people enjoyed working with him and that by planning, communicating and working with them, he was becoming not only more successful, but he also truly enjoyed what he was doing at a much higher level.

As a coach, it is never my job to tell people what to do, it is my job to help them identify the actions and behaviors they believe will work for them and assist them in achieving their goals. Bill needed to decide where to focus, and he had to commit to shifting his behavior. Finally the changes he elected to make needed to be authentic. People are very good at seeing through manipulative behavior, and it rarely results in sustainable results.

The role of Area Sales Director is still on the horizon for Bill, but his early missteps definitely had affected his ability to achieve his desired outcome in the timeframe he would have liked. One of his stakeholders is now his mentor, and he is getting more support from his peers. His retention numbers are improving, and while it is too early for another 360, the indications are that there will be improvement there as well. Whether Bill will get the promotion is not clear; it is sometimes difficult to overcome a reputation you have created, but it won't be for lack of trying. If the promotion goes to someone else, Bill might decide to move on, but what he has learned in the process will undoubtedly have a beneficial outcome on his next opportunity.

It is worth the effort to focus on your career early; as Bill experienced, a lack of attention and doing what we have always done will not usually get us to the next level. Overcoming a false start at any company and in any role can cost you more than just a missed promotion, it can waste time and deplete your energy, and it can definitely limit your potential. Career management is critical not only to your ultimate success, but to giving you the level of satisfaction and fulfillment you deserve.

Managing Your Career

When I talk to individuals or groups about career management, I'm often asked why they need a career management plan if they are not focused on promotions or moving ahead. The answer is both simple in concept and complex in execution. A plan for managing your career is key to ensuring that the many hours you spend at work is fulfilling and meets your needs.

Start by understanding what will make you successful in your career. Through the years, I've gathered a list of time-proven factors to create and enhance a successful career:

- *Seek and get help:* Consider finding a mentor. This can be someone in the organization, or someone you trust from another area of your life.
- *Create a track record of success:* Understand that demonstrating success and top performance in your current role is critical. Be sure you know the expectations of the new role (and from your new boss), and focus on exceeding expectations. This is a ticket to play if you

ever want to move up, or be considered for any other role in the organization.

✦ *Demonstrate a desire to succeed:* Let people know that you are fully focused on success and that you want to progress in your career. Ask for feedback on your performance, then listen and respond to suggestions for improvement.

✦ *Successfully manage relationships:* Organizations are successful based on the work of many individuals and teams. You must be able to demonstrate that you can build successful relationships and that you can work well in a team environment.

✦ *Be willing to take career risks:* There will be times when you need to make bold decisions— and take action. Of course, always consider the organizational culture and political expectations to determine the appropriate actions to take.

✦ *Ability to be tough, decisive and demanding:* Be prepared to take a stand, make decisions and move forward. While building consensus and collaborating are important attributes for a leader, you must always be prepared to make tough decisions when appropriate.

✦ *Emotional Intelligence:* Thinking on your feet and being able to "get along" in the organization's culture are the keys to success. There are many resources available to assist you in building your emotional intelligence—start with some of the free assessments online.

- *Presence:* This is sometimes called "executive presence," but at any level in an organization you need to know how to "show up." People will look at how you behave in meetings, how you make presentations, and how you present your position in a variety of situations.
- *Fitting in:* In the world of career transition, we often say, "You are hired for your skills, talents and abilities, and you are fired for your inability to fit in." Take time to understand the culture of the organization and determine how to do your work and fulfill your role within the expectations of the culture.
- *Influence versus control:* To survive in an organization, you will often need to work through others to accomplish objectives. This can be challenging when the "others" do not report to you. You need to work on influencing others to assist you in meeting your objectives.

It's Your Turn

If you are in a current role or job, take a few minutes and write down how you think you are doing in each of these areas. If you don't know, ask some of your co-workers:

Help from others—A mentor, do you have one?:

___

Track record of success:

_____
_____
_____
_____
_____
_____
_____
_____
_____

Demonstrate a desire to succeed:

_____
_____
_____
_____
_____
_____
_____
_____
_____
_____

Ability to manage relationships:

Willingness to take career risks:

Ability to be tough, decisive and demanding:

Emotional Intelligence:

Presence:

Fitting in:

Influencing:

If you are in a current role or position, your organization may have a career management template. If you do not have such a tool, here are some basic components to include:

- ✦ *What is your desired outcome?* Determine what you want to achieve at this point in your career. Go back and consider the five career positions we discussed earlier, in Chapter 2, *Where Are You in Your Career?* Depending upon where you believe you are at this point, define the outcome. For example, if you are in the center, *Enhance*, what specifically do you want as an outcome? It may be that you want additional training opportunities, certifications or projects.

If you are in the *Deceleration Position,* you need to know if you want to exit for good, or for a specific amount of time. What do you want now and what is the ultimate outcome? For example, "I want to take three years off, and then return to this job, company or industry."

✦ *When will it be complete?* As you determine the outcome you want, put a time limit on accomplishing it. If it is a certification, work directly toward the steps to achieve it.

✦ *What is the importance to the organization or team?* While managing your career is important to your ultimate career success, you need to make sure that what you are working toward accomplishing is also in alignment with organizational objectives. For example, if you are in Upward Mobility, what more can you contribute or deliver as you move up?

✦ *How will it be accomplished?* You may need additional resources or assistance from others to achieve your career objectives. Be clear about what you need and the steps you will take to reach your goals. This is setting your strategy.

✦ *Who can provide assistance to you?* Define the people that can help you move toward your career goals. It may be your boss, someone from another organization or team, someone in another department of your organization, or perhaps someone from outside.

✦ *How will you measure success?* Be clear about knowing when you have arrived. Those moments are marked by milestones such as when you get your certification, or new projects you are assigned and successfully complete. If you are in *Deceleration*, you may have multiple milestones, the first is negotiating your new role or time off, staying current or connected to your desired outcome, and finally, returning to or achieving your ultimate outcome.

It's Your Turn

Take a few minutes and write down how you think you are doing in each of these areas:

What is your desired outcome?

_____
_____
_____
_____
_____
_____
_____
_____
_____
_____

When will it be complete?

What is the importance to the organization or team?

How will it be accomplished?

Who can provide assistance to you?

How will you measure success?

Transition Point

Once you have determined the objectives of your career, check in periodically with the tools identified to ensure that you are making progress. A measure of progress must include the conviction that you continue to be fulfilled and energized!

Transition Points

CHAPTER 7

*I have learned, that if one advances confidently
in the direction of his dreams, and endeavors
to live the life he has imagined, he will meet with
a success unexpected in common hours.*
Henry David Thoreau

A career is a series of Transition Points. Unfortunately, people often do not recognize that they are at such a point and they fail to make an intentional choice. Instead, they give up much of the control they could have over that next step in the course of their own career. This book is all about taking charge of your career and making intentional transitions.

For the past 15 years I have studied how people make transitions. One thing is very clear to me:

> You can make a choice about how you will respond to events and people in your life. If you do not make a conscious choice—an intentional choice—a decision will be made for you by someone or something else. It *is* your choice—your decision—to make the transition.

The following is a summary of the Transition Points we have talked about that you have in your career:

Transition Point #1

You spend many of your waking hours working. It is up to you how those hours are spent. By taking control of your career, it is possible to create the career of your dreams.

Take time to consider how you are spending your time at work. I have worked with far too many people who have spent sometimes 20 plus years in a career or doing something they do not really like. Many of these people have even achieved great success ... but they are empty and unfulfilled. Start thinking now about how you choose to spend your time. It really is a choice *you* can make at any point in your career. It is never too early and it is never too late.

Transition Point #2

Few actually think about or create a career map. Some simply get lost, or worse, don't know they are lost; some just wander around; some just plow ahead, never even thinking about it; some just coat tail onto someone else's "career map," not really conscious of what they are doing. And some are directed by another's career choice for them.

But, it is your career map, not someone else's.

It's not unusual to be in limbo during your working years. Knowing where you are, right now, allows you to determine where you want to go.

There are at least five different places you may be in your career at any given time. Don't allow yourself to get stuck in any one of those places because as you change and your life changes, your career aspirations or desires change too. Too often we identify so strongly with our image of where we should be that we don't allow ourselves to acknowledge and embrace where we actually are, or where we want to be.

Take the time to think about the changes in your life and your desires—re-plot your place on the Career Position Model in Chapter 2, *Where Are You in Your Career.* Try not to make value judgments about where you are. All of the places are viable, necessary and part of your career evolution.

Transition Point #3

It is impossible to mentally and physically move forward without knowing where you are, what you want, where you want to go and why you want to get there. It is your "come to career" moment.

> Too often we do not consider what we really want from a career. Acknowledging and prioritizing your true career or job needs and wants will position you to make high quality and sustainable choices throughout your career. Understanding what and why things are important to you also positions you to successfully negotiate for the important things, and not to get sidetracked with "shiny" objects that are dangled before you in a job search or career change.

Transition Point #4

Now that you have a sense of what you are good at and what you love doing, it is time to consider how to manage The Career Connection Quadrants *depending upon your situation. Simply put, do you want to make a real change to a new career, or short of that, still want to increase your fulfillment and satisfaction within your current career?*

> There is an old adage, "If you have been so successful at something you don't truly love, just think about how successful you could be if you were doing something you *really love*."

This should be the guiding light in making and managing your career choices. Understanding your Four Quadrants will enable you to manage the frustrations and joys of your career.

Transition Point #5

Regardless of where you are in your career—making a change or enhancing your current role—it is your responsibility to own your choices and how you respond to any event or situation. Always remember, you do have significant control over the outcomes you create because you chose the response.

E + R → O

In the absence of intentional choices, it is easy to become a "victim" of your own career. Recognize that *you own your choices*. If you are not pleased with the current outcomes of your career or job, it is up to you to make conscious changes to move closer to what you really want.

Transition Point #6

Once you have determined the objectives of your career, check in periodically with the tools identified to ensure that you are making progress, and that you continue to be fulfilled and energized!

Managing your career never ends. Whether you are starting a new job, moving up or decelerating your career, it is up to you to proactively manage the outcome. Don't get too comfortable in any role or position. Recognize that you are always being evaluated, compared to others and assessed on your performance.

Summing Up

Change is what happens ... it happens every day throughout your career. *Transition* is how you make the choices and respond to all the changes, being fully conscious, aware and intentional with the choices you select. Whether in your career or your life, this waking up and taking ownership becomes your *TransitionPoint*. It's never too early; it's never too late.

Starting today, determine:

- What you are good at, but don't love;
- What you are not good at and don't love;
- What you love, but you are not good at yet; and
- What you love and what you are really good at.

I hope by working with these tools, you find your Career Intersection of Skill and Passion. It is an ever changing dynamic, but understanding it and making more intentional choices will give you so much joy and fulfillment that you truly will say, "Wow, and they pay me to do this!"

Final Word

As I wrote TransitionPoints, I reflected often on my own career experiences, as well as those of the people with whom I have had the privilege to work. It occurred to me that while often people would tell me they had been opportunistic about their careers, they all shared one thing in common. They all had an internal sense, though sometimes far off on the horizon, of what they really wanted in life and in work. The issue was always that in the hustle and bustle of daily living, they never really focused on that *something*. Consequently, it got lost in the shuffle. They often became frustrated, anxious, or just uncomfortable with not knowing specifically what or where they wanted to go at a given time.

My intent is to support you in remembering, discovering and focusing on your intersection of excellence and passion. If you are just starting out after completing your degree, or just joining the workforce, get in touch with your passions and make the connection to what you do really well, it will save you years of *wandering* through jobs and ending up wasting years in jobs or companies that may feed your belly but will starve your soul. If you are at a midpoint in your career, slow down and take the time for *you* this time. You have likely spent your career and much of your life taking care of others and losing your own intentions and passions in the process.

You may use this book as a *reminder* to reconnect with your passion. You may even *find* your passion and *acknowledge* the concepts and use them to *clarify* your direction.

Regardless of how you use the processes defined, I can tell you from experience that they are a powerful way to get yourself focused and to honor your passions, skills and talents.

I wish you great success in your life and in your career and promise you…

When you find the work you do well and truly love, you will never work another day in your life.

About the Author

Nancy Sullivan started her career in 1980, directly out of college, as a management hire for what was then Mountain Bell Telephone. Recognized early as an emerging leader, she was consistently promoted and was able to expand her resume to include roles in New Product Development, Video, Multi-Media, Customer Experience and Network Special Services Repair and Installation. During this career, Nancy also managed teams at many levels and was awarded the President's Club status year after year.

In the late '90s, she became certified with William Bridges and Associates, the godfather of change, and transitioned the skills and insights learned from this giant to her work with the firm Lee Hecht Harrison (LHH). Certifying as an Executive Coach and as a Board Certified Coach allowed Nancy to coach at multiple levels—from engineers and physicians to CEOs.

Nancy has also been a volunteer with multiple hospice organizations, learning through firsthand experience about the most important transition anyone will face personally. This experience has enabled her to work with both families and patients, coaching them through the challenges and new awakenings this final transition presents.

Transitions are what Nancy Sullivan is all about. The love of them, the fear of them, and the growth from them. The insights that she brings to any conference, workshop or private coaching session are based on her many hundreds of global interviews and work with people experiencing every kind of change.

To bring Nancy to your organization, have her speak at your conference or consult with her, email:

Nancy@NancySullivanAuthor.com

TransitionPoints@gmail.com

NancySullivanAuthor.com

Working with Nancy Sullivan

Nancy is a widely known speaker and executive coach, continuing to support teams, organizations and individuals to work through transitions of all kinds.

If you would like to have Nancy speak at an event for your organization, or to your team, or if you would like to work individually with her as a coach, you can reach her at **TransitionPoints@gmail.com**.

Clients Are Talking

Nancy spoke on the topic of Career Management to our organization. With an audience of 1500, we got the highest evaluations for quality and satisfaction. Nancy hit the mark not only for the entry level team members, but also for our senior level leaders.

—John M., CEO

I worked with Nancy as my coach and learned how to navigate through some of the most challenging times in preparation for a long desired promotion. With Nancy's help, I was promoted to the job of my dreams!

—Joan T., SVP